TeeLee GETS THE WORD OUT

an advertising book

by

Adam Palmeter

Wow, TeeLee! Looks like you have a great little PIGGY BUN business! How's it going?
Hey Mr. Feefers! It's going pretty well, thanks!
TeeLee's PiGGY BUNs
SOLD OUT!
1

friends!
friends!
I've been selling them to my friends, but I wish I could sell more!
You need to GET THE WORD OUT and find more CUSTOMERS to buy your buns!
2

Exactly, Mr. FeeFers! But how can I let more CUSTOMERS know about my BUNS?
customer: someone who buys a product or service.
noun
3

Maybe you can try ADVERTISING for your BUNS!
What's ADVERTISING, Mr. FeeFers?
4

Many customers dont know about your product yet.
ADVERTISING lets them know!

ad·ver·tise
verb
:to describe or draw attention to a product, service, or event.

WOW!
More customers!
How can I advertise
for my Piggy Buns?

Well, TeeLee,
You can ADVERTISE
many ways...

6

Giving out
FREE SAMPLES
is a delicious way to
let customers try
your new product!
FREE!
7

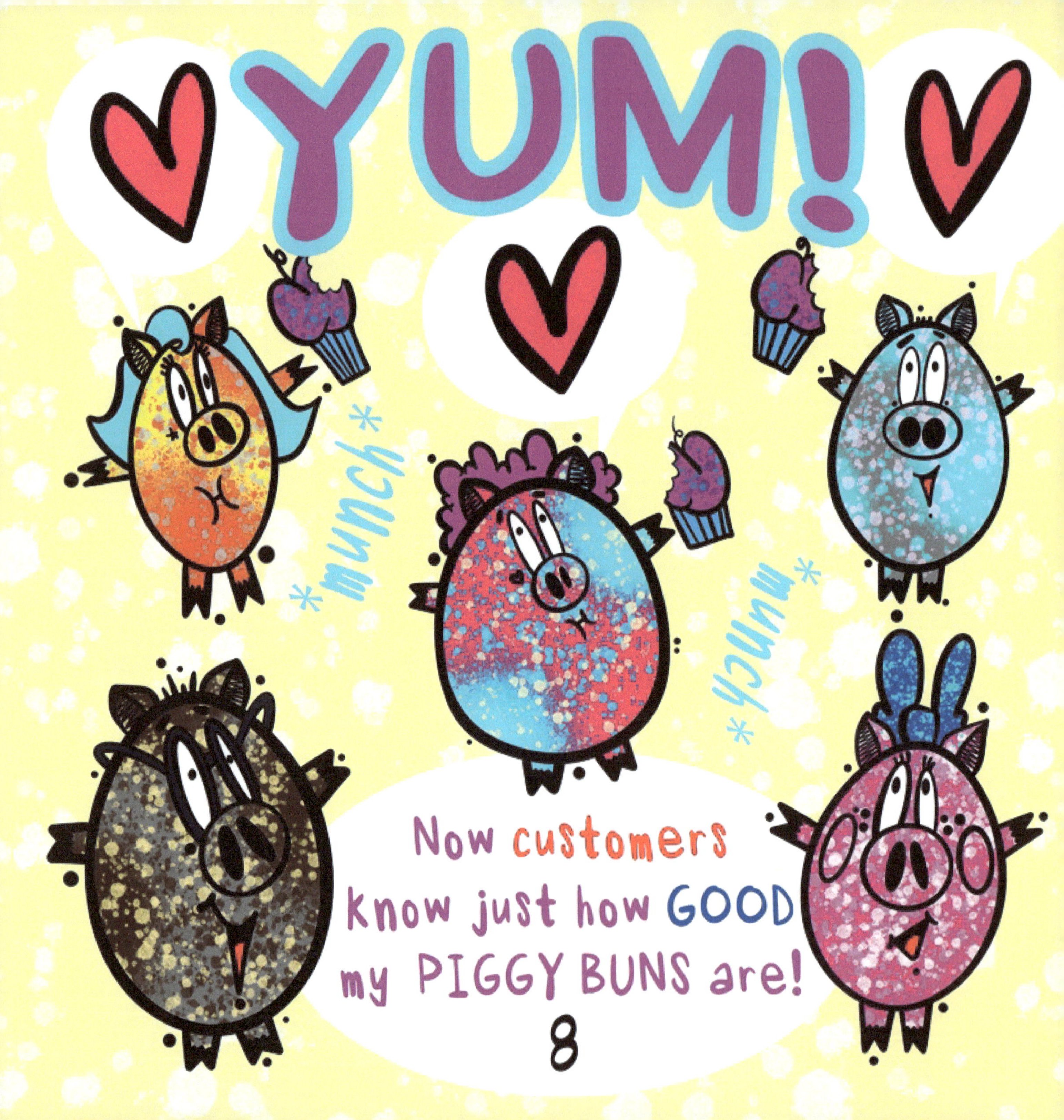
YUM!
munch
munch
munch
Now customers know just how GOOD my PIGGY BUNS are!
8

♡!
Then they tell all their friends about your buns! That's "WORD OF MOUTH!"
9

Troy advertises with COUPONS for half-price books at his book store. That's another way to find new customers!
TROY STORY
book store
50% OFF one BOOK!
10

TEELEE'S
PIGGY BUNS
Making a cool
POSTER
can help you get a lot
of new attention!
11

Then put the posters where everyone can see them!
That way everyone will know about my BUNS!
TEELEE's PIGGY BUNS
12

TEE LEE's
PIGGY BUNS
TEE LEE's
PIGGY BUNS
You could
even advertise online
right to customers'
phones and
computers, BUT
you will need
a grown-up
PIG to help
you do that!
13

Having an
EVENT or PERFORMANCE
is a fun way to attract
customers as well!
14

YUP!
Like when Juli da' Harper performs at the Pop Shop!
Pop's Slop - Pop Shop
15

You could hire
TED & the 3P
Dance-
-CroBats
to perform for your customers!
16

Yeah! I'm a total TEDHEAD! My friends and I LOVE the 3P Dance-CroBats!
ME TOO! They have many fans. If you hired them to perform, it would be a great OPPORTUNITY to sell their fans PIGGY BUNS!
17

These are all great ways to ADVERTISE!
Now you can really find more customers to buy your PIGGY BUNS!
18

With all these new customers buying PIGGY BUNS, business will really be BOOMING!
19

ADVERTISING can be a lot of hard work, but hard work can really pay off!
Looks like it's up to me to GET THE WORD OUT about my Piggy Buns...
TEELEE's PIGGY BUNS
TEELEE's PIGGY BUNS
20

...and I'm getting some pretty SWEET ideas, Mr. FeeFeers! Time for me to get to work!
Good Luck, TeeLee!
21

TeeLee's
PiGGY BUNs
$2

the end

www.Opportuni-tree.com

About the Author:

Adam Palmeter is an author, visual artist, international stand up comedian, entrepreneur, and teacher of students of all ages across New York, South Korea, Vietnam and China.

@AdamPalmeter

www.ingramcontent.com/pod-product-compliance
Lightning Source LLC
Chambersburg PA
CBHW042140030726
47599CB00002B/550